This book is to be returned on or before
the last date stamped below.

Look After Yourself
Keep Healthy!

Angela Royston

Heinemann
LIBRARY

www.heinemann.co.uk/library
Visit our website to find out more information about **Heinemann Library** books.

To order:
☎ Phone 44 (0) 1865 888066
🖷 Send a fax to 44 (0) 1865 314091
🖵 Visit the Heinemann Bookshop at www.heinemann.co.uk/library to browse our
catalogue and order online.

First published in Great Britain by Heinemann
Library, Halley Court, Jordan Hill, Oxford
OX2 8EJ, part of Harcourt Education.
Heinemann is a registered trademark of Harcourt
Education Ltd.

Editorial: Sarah Eason and Kathy Peltan
Design: Dave Oakley, Arnos Design
Picture Research: Helen Reilly, Arnos Design
Production: Edward Moore

Originated by Dot Gradations Ltd
Printed and bound in Hong Kong and China by
South China

ISBN 0 431 18027 X
07 06 05 04 03
10 9 8 7 6 5 4 3 2 1

**British Library Cataloguing in Publication
Data**
Royston, Angela
Keep healthy. – (Look after yourself)
1.Health – Juvenile literature
I.Title
613

A full catalogue record for this book is available
from the British Library.

Acknowledgements
The publishers would like to thank the following
for permission to reproduce photographs:
Bubbles p.**5** (Loisjoy Thurston), p.**26** (Paul
Howard); Gareth Boden p.**10**; Getty Images p.**12**
(Joseph Devenney), p.**18** (Bruce Ayres), p.**21**
(Vincent Oliver); p.**22** (Chronis Johs), p.**24** Arthur
Tilley; Science Photo Library p.**7** (Eye of Science);
p.**13** (Gusto), p.**23** Gaillard, Jerrican), p.**25**
(BSIP/Laurent), p.**27** (Saturn Stills); Trevor Clifford
pp.**8**, **9**, **11**, **14**, **15**, **16**, **17**, **19**, **20**; Trip p.**4** (G.
Lennox), p.**6** (H. Rogers).

Cover photograph reproduced with permission of
Bubbles/Angela Hampton.

The publishers would like to thank David Wright
for his assistance in the preparation of this book.

Every effort has been made to contact copyright
holders of any material reproduced in this book.
Any omissions will be rectified in subsequent
printings if notice is given to the publishers.

Contents

Words written in bold, **like this**, are explained in the Glossary.

Your body

Your body is like an amazing machine. It has many different parts that work together. If **germs** get inside your body, they can stop some of the parts from working properly.

For example, if germs get into your stomach, they may make you feel sick. This book tells you how you can help to stop germs getting inside your body.

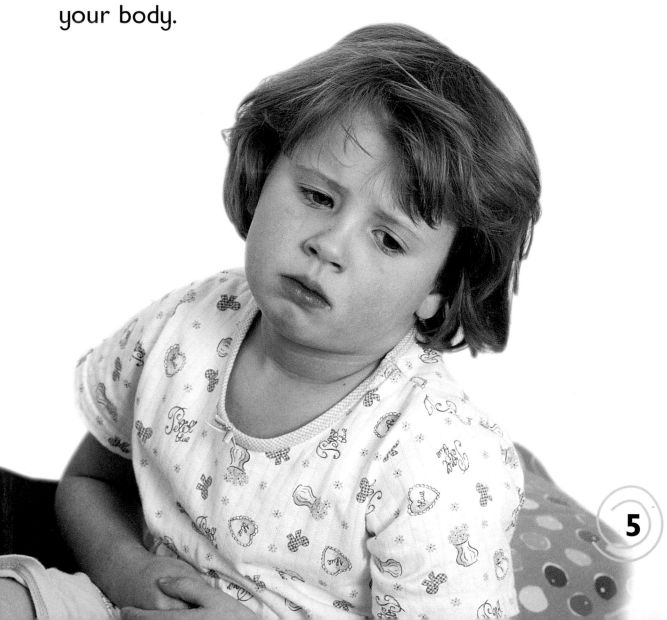

What are germs?

Germs are **bacteria**, **viruses** or **fungi**. Some germs get into your body with the air you breathe. Others get in with your food.

Germs can only be seen through a **microscope**, because they are so small. This is what the virus that causes a **disease** called chickenpox looks like through a microscope.

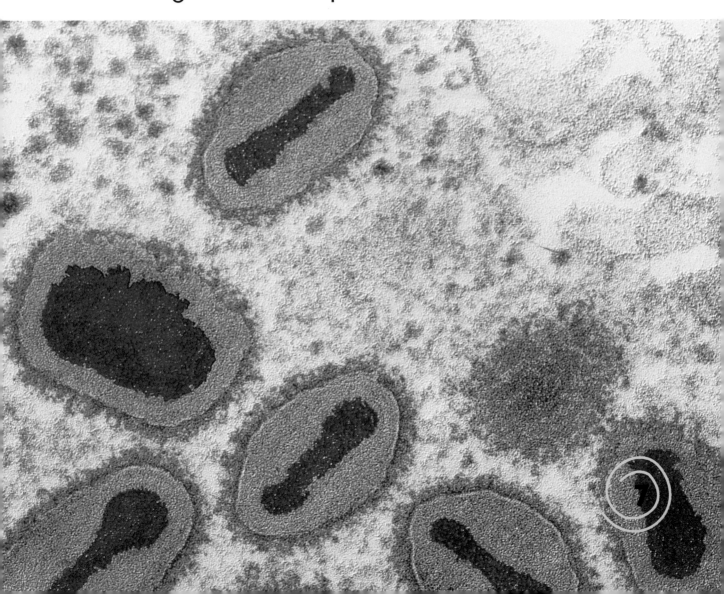

Take care of cuts

If you cut or graze your skin, **germs** can get inside your body through the cut or graze. Ask an adult to help you clean the wound with water.

Use a special cream to kill any germs. When the wound is clean, cover it with a plaster. The plaster will stop more germs getting in through the cut.

Avoid sharing towels

Some **germs** make your eyes red and sore. You can catch germs from someone else's towel. You rub the germs into your eyes when you dry your face.

Other germs affect your skin, particularly the skin on your feet. If you have germs on your skin, they will rub off on to your towel. Keep your germs to yourself – don't share your towel!

Wash your hands

Soap and water wash **germs** off your skin. Make sure you wash your hands after using the toilet. Always wash your hands before you eat.

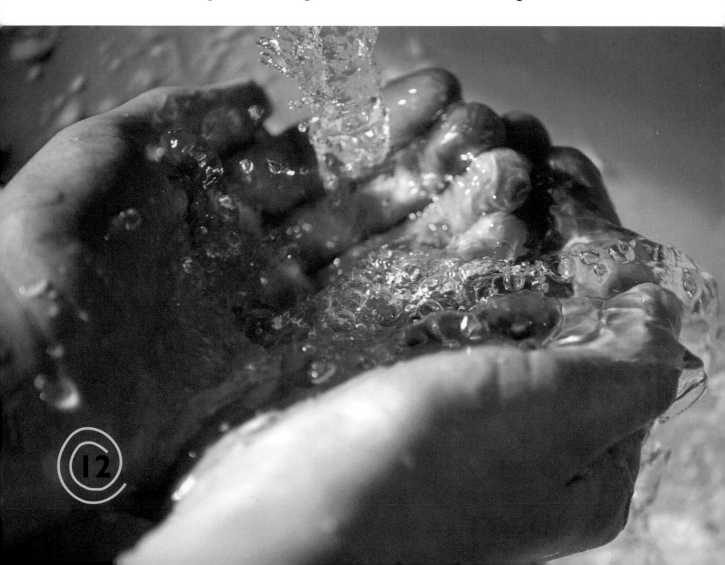

If you do not wash your hands, germs can spread to your food. When you eat the food, the germs go into your body and can make you ill.

Eat safe food

Food can carry **germs** too. Make sure that the food you eat is clean and fresh. Wash cherries, strawberries and other fruits before you eat them.

When food has been kept too long, it begins to smell bad and taste odd. It may also look **mouldy**. Do not eat food like this.

Germs in the air

Some **germs** spread through the air. Coughing and sneezing release germs into the air. Cover your nose and mouth when you sneeze. Cover your mouth when you cough.

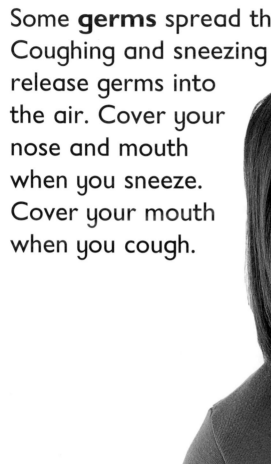

Covering your nose and mouth helps to stop the germs spreading to other people. When you have blown your nose on a tissue, do not leave the tissue lying around. Put it in a bin.

Treating fever

This girl is having her **temperature** taken. Her body is hotter than usual because she has **flu**. The high temperature makes her feel very ill.

When you have a temperature, you can help your body to cool down. Drink plenty of water. Sponging your skin with water helps, too.

Take your medicine

You may need to take some **medicine** to help you get better. It is important to follow the instructions exactly. Do not take more medicine than you should. This can be very dangerous.

Also do not take less medicine than the **doctor** tells you to take. You should keep taking some medicines, even if you are feeling better.

Going to the doctor

Sometimes your body needs help to get better. A **doctor** may need to examine you to see what is wrong. The doctor will look down your throat.

Then she will listen to your chest as you cough. She uses an instrument called a **stethoscope** to help her hear better. She may also examine your ears.

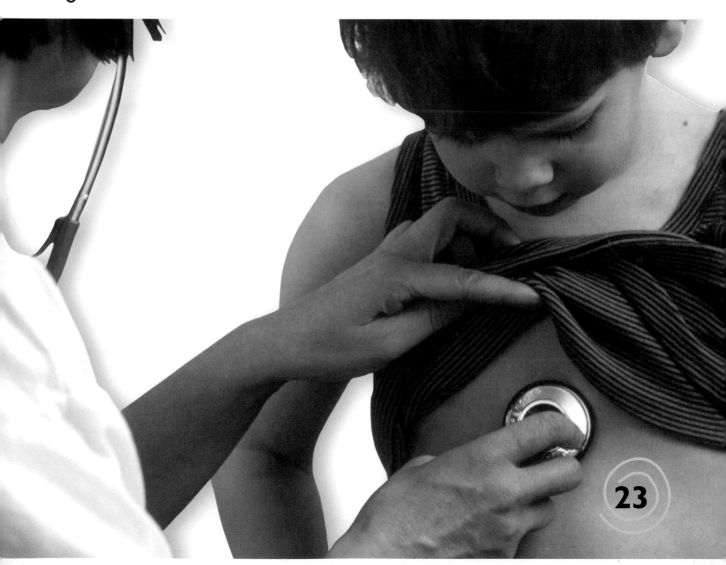

23

Medical checks

Young children need to have a medical check every few years. The **doctor** or **nurse** will check how well you can see and hear.

You will also be weighed and your
height will be measured.
The doctor checks that
your weight and height
are right for
your age.

Vaccinations

Vaccinations stop you getting some dangerous illnesses. Babies are made to swallow drops that will protect them from a **disease** called polio.

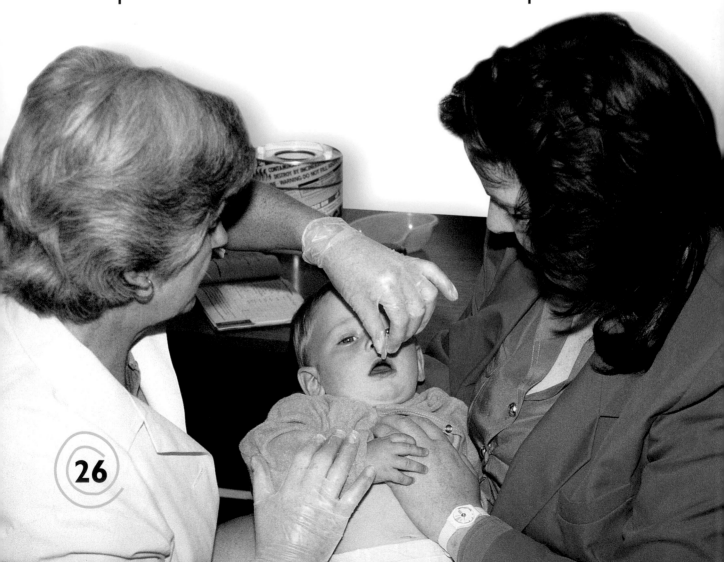

Babies are also given **injections**. The injections contain **vaccines** that will protect them from diseases such as measles.

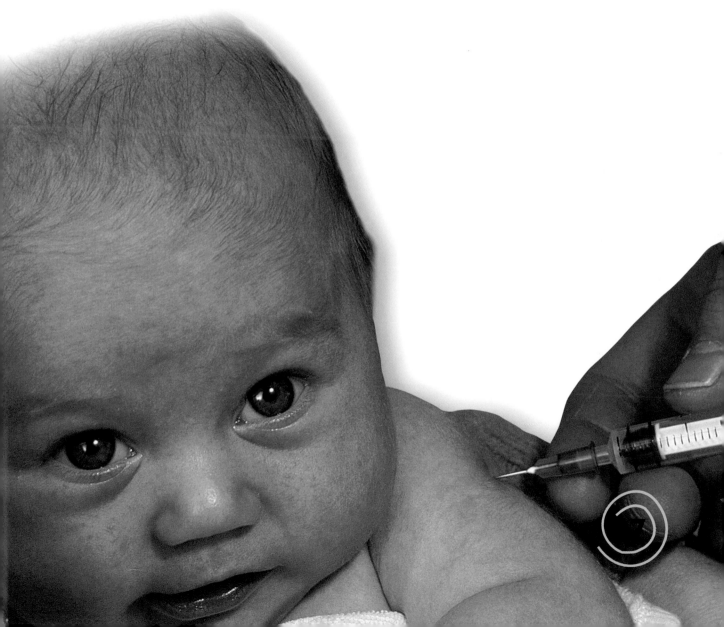

You cannot avoid **germs** by looking out for them. Germs are so small you cannot see them – 8000 germs laid side by side would measure just a centimetre.

Germs quickly produce more germs. Some germs can double in number every 20 minutes. This means that a group of 100 germs can grow to 200 germs after 20 minutes, 400 germs after 40 minutes, and 800 germs after an hour.

Bacteria can live in your body. Most of them live on your skin, in your mouth, in your stomach and in your **intestines**. Many also live in the tubes that link your nose and lungs.

Antibiotics are special medicines that kill some bacteria in the body.

Your body kills germs in many different ways. For example, **saliva** in your mouth can kill some germs. Special cells in your blood kill off most of the germs that get inside your body.

When you sneeze, air and germs are forced out of your nose and mouth very fast. They travel as fast as a car on the motorway! This means that they can spread to everyone in the same room as you.

Glossary

antibiotic   medicine that fights bacteria

bacteria   tiny living things – some kinds of bacteria can make you ill if they get inside your body

disease   an illness

doctor   person who knows how to treat illnesses and other things that may go wrong with the body

flu   illness like a very bad cold, but often with a fever

fungus (plural fungi)   group of living things that includes some germs but also useful foods such as mushrooms and yeast

germs   tiny living things that attack different parts of your body. Bacteria, viruses and fungi are germs.

injection   when a small amount of fluid is pushed through a hollow needle into the body

intestines   long tube in the body that food goes through after it leaves the stomach

medicine   substance used to treat an illness

microscope   instrument that makes very small things look large enough to see

mould a kind of fungus that forms as a green or white substance on old food

nurse person who is trained to look after people who are ill or injured

saliva liquid made in the mouth to help you chew and swallow food

stethoscope instrument that allows a doctor or nurse to listen to the sound of your heart beating and your lungs breathing

temperature a measure of how hot or cold something is

vaccine substance that prevents you getting a particular disease

vaccination injection of vaccine into the body

virus a kind of germ

Find out more

Essentials: Keeping Healthy by John Foster (Collins Educational, 2003)

My Amazing Body: A First Look at Health and Fitness by Pat Thomas and Lesley Harker (Hodder Wayland, 2002)

Safe and Sound: Clean and Healthy by Angela Royston (Heinemann Library, 2000)

Safe and Sound: Healthy Body by Angela Royston (Heinemann Library, 2000)